SONGS of the 20's

THE DECADE SERIES

PIANO • VOCAL • GUITAR

P9-CEI-328

HAL•LEONARD® CORPORATION

7777 W. BLUEMOUND RD. P.O. BOX 13819 MILWAUKEE, WI 53213

The Twenties

by Stanley Green

The Seattle Daily Times

SEATTLE, WASHINGTON, SUNDAY MORNING, MAY 22, 1927.

LINDBERGH IN PARIS!
50,000 CHEER U. S. FLYER

It began with the crisp martial blare of soldiers returning home from World War I and ended with the mournful wail of the Wall Street debacle. In between, the Roaring Twenties were the years of F. Scott Fitzgerald novels and John Held Jr. cartoons, of Silent Cal in the White House and Lucky Lindy winging his lonely way across the Atlantic, of Man o' War on the turf and Rudolph Valentino, Mary Pickford, Douglas Fairbanks, Charlie Chaplin, and Rin-Tin-Tin on the silver screen. It was a period dominated by the noble experiment known as Prohibition, which may have failed to enforce alcoholic temperence but which did succeed in fostering bootlegging, speakeasies, moonshining, and mob violence personified by the menacing figure of Al Capone. It had sports heroes dubbed the Manassa Mauler, the Sultan of Swat, and the Galloping Ghost, and it offered a variety of fads and fashions, as flappers bobbed their hair and raised their skirts, and lounge lizards sported raccoon coats and baggy pants, strummed ukuleles and banjos, and drank from hip flasks. It was, in short, the period that columnist Westbrook Pegler called "the era of wonderful nonsense."

NEW YORK, WEDNESDAY, NOVEMBER 3, 1920.

HARDING WINS; MILLION LEAD HERE;
BIG REPUBLICAN GAINS IN CONGRESS;
MILLER LEADS SMITH FOR GOVERNOR

*A*nother name for it was The Jazz Age, though the term was used less as a musical designation than to describe the decade's revolt against traditional, morals and mores. Just as the spontaneous sound of jazz broke loose from the more accepted musical forms of the past, so the spontaneous reaction to the bloody war that had just ended — and as an expression of the nation's carefree spirit during a period of economic growth — was to turn many away from long-held strictures of behavior. Thus it was only right that jazz should add the beat, the contagious ragtime meter to the mainstream of popular music as it filled the demand of a high-stepping, uninhibited society.

*T*he optimistic spirit of the decade was neatly summed up in a bit of quack psychotherapy propounded by Dr. Emile Coué — "Day by day, in every way, I'm getting better and better." Not only did people feel that their lives could be improved by simplistic autosuggestion, there was a general attitude — expressed in the popular songs of the day — that unhappiness was only temporary and that any setback could be easily overcome. We were told that April showers bring May flowers. That there would be no more sobbin' when the red, red robin comes bob, bob, bobbin' along. That when you're smiling, the whole world smiles at you. That all you need on a rainy day is to let a smile be your umbrella.

It should also be noted that most of the so-called jazz songs of the period were more razzmatazz than real jazz. Still, there was no question that the syncopated beat was much in evidence in such infectious pieces as "Baby Face," "Five Foot Two, Eyes of Blue," and "Everybody Loves My Baby." Some numbers even addressed themselves directly to the new rhythm, such as "Crazy Rhythm," which offered the observation, "What's the use of Prohibition? You produce the same condition." There was, however, a more authentic jazz sound in the songs written and performed by black writers and entertainers. In 1929, Louis Armstrong took over Fats Waller's "Ain't Misbehavin'" when he was appearing in the Broadway show *Hot Chocolates* and turned it into a trademark number. Ethel Waters did the same for "There'll Be Some Changes Made," one of her earliest recordings. And the black vaudeville team of Henry Creamer and Turner Layton introduced their own tribute to the cradle of jazz, "'Way Down Yonder In New Orleans."

Since jazz was king in the Twenties, there had to be a King of Jazz. Ever since first arriving in New York in 1920 to appear at the Palais Royale nightclub, the undisputed crown-wearer was a rotund orchestra leader named Paul Whiteman. Whiteman's brand of orchestral — even symphonic — jazz may not have been for the purists, but it did help to popularize the form as well as to elevate the entire field of American dance music. Among the Whiteman specialties were such numbers as the blues novelty "Wang Wang Blues," the romantic "In A Little Spanish Town," the dreaming "Among My Souvenirs," and the Fats Waller-Andy Razaf "Honeysuckle Rose." Another song, the foot-stomping "Mississippi Mud," was more than an orchestra specialty, since it also served to introduce audiences to a vocal trio known as the Rhythm Boys, one of whom was a 24-year-old crooner from Tacoma named Bing Crosby.

Paul Whiteman and his Orchestra

Rhythm Boys

The Twenties also saw the emergence of other topflight bands that introduced and popularized many of the lasting hits of the decade. "'Deed I Do" was identified with the "Ol' Maestro" Ben Bernie ("Yowzah, yowzah"), while "Me And My Shadow," "When My Sugar Walks Down The Street," "Star Dust," and "Sugar Blues" were associated with, respectively, Ted Lewis, Phil Harris, Isham Jones, and Clyde McCoy. In 1929, crooning idol Rudy Vallee fronted a dance band known as the Connecticut Yankees and turned a thirteen-year-old English ballad, "If You Were The Only Girl In The World," into a hit in the United States.

The leading entertainer of the decade was the dynamic Al Jolson, who wore blackface makeup, dropped to one knee and flung out his arms as he vowed to walk a million miles for one of his Mammy's smiles. Even in his Broadway shows, Jolson always interpolated his own specialties, such as "April Showers" and "California, Here I Come" in *Bombo* (1921), and "If You Knew Susie Like I Know Susie" and "It All Depends On You" in *Big Boy* (1925).

Al Jolson

Eddie Cantor

Probably Jolson's closest rival as a song-and-dance attraction was the energetic, eye-popping Eddie Cantor, who originally billed himself as "The Apostle of Pep." Cantor's repertory included such songs as "Ma! He's Making Eyes At Me" (sung in *The Midnight Rounders*), "Baby Face," and "If You Knew Susie," which though introduced by Jolson, became far more closely identified with Cantor. Another Cantor specialty, "Yes! We Have No Bananas," caused more of a sensation in the Twenties than any other novelty number. Actually, it was a patchwork song made up by stringing together five recognizable themes: the "Hallelujah" chorus from Handel's "Messiah," the last line from "My Bonnie Lies Over The Ocean," the middle part of "I Dreamt That I Dwelt In Marble Halls," the line "I was seeing Nellie home" from "Aunt Dinah's Quilting Party," and Cole Porter's "An Old Fashioned Garden."

*A*part from phonographs and Broadway shows, the chief area for introducing popular songs in the Twenties was vaudeville which, for a modest price, offered audiences variety bills consisting of just about every form of entertainment — from song-and-dance performers to acrobats, from comedy sketches to dramatic scenes, from animal acts to operatic excerpts. Among headliners of the decade were torch singer Ruth Etting (who introduced "Mean To Me"), chirpy-voiced Cliff "Ukulele Ike" Edwards ("I Cried For You" and "Paddlin' Madelin' Home"), the harmonizing duo of Van and Schenck ("Who's Sorry Now?"), the singing and dancing Duncan Sisters ("Let A Smile Be Your Umbrella" and "Side By Side"), and Sophie Tucker, billed as "The Last Of The Red Hot Mamas" ("When The Red, Red Robin Comes Bob, Bob, Bobbin' Along").

Florenz Ziegfeld

Jerome Kern

*U*nquestionably, however, it was Broadway that provided the most prestigious outlet for the most glittering stars and the most accomplished composers and lyricists. It was also the domain of the legendary Florenz Ziegfeld, who presided over seven editions of his celebrated *Follies* revue during the decade. Especially notable was the 1921 production in which comedienne Fanny Brice introduced the seriocomic lament "Second Hand Rose." Ziegfeld also sponsored two major book shows of the Twenties: Jerome Kern's *Sally* starring Marilyn Miller (who sang the memorable "Look For The Silver Lining") and another Kern musical, the classic *Show Boat*, written with Oscar Hammerstein II (whence came the tender "Make Believe" and the powerful "Ol' Man River").

The Twenties were also significant for introducing many of the creative giants of the musical theatre. Richard Rodgers and Lorenz Hart enjoyed their first Broadway success in 1925 with *The Garrick Gaieties*, which included the durable "Sentimental Me" and "Manhattan." Composer Vincent Youmans, who made his Broadway bow in 1921, wrote "Hallelujah!" for *Hit The Deck!* and "More Than You Know" for *Great Day!* Jimmy McHugh and Dorothy Fields attracted notice with their first show, *Blackbirds Of 1928*, whose most popular number was the confession of an impecunious swain, "I Can't Give You Anything But Love." And the triad of B.G. DeSylva, Lew Brown and Ray Henderson caught the spirit of the decade's flaming youth with such songs as "The Varsity Drag" in *Good News!*, "You're The Cream In My Coffee" in *Hold Everything!* and "Button Up Your Overcoat" in *Follow Thru.*

Though sound on film had been demonstrated as early as 1900 at the Paris International Exposition, the first feature-length motion pictures with a musical background score did not come along until 1926 with the release of *Don Juan*, starring John Barrymore. That was followed by another silent film with musical accompaniment, *What Price Glory*, which gave us our first theme song in Erno Rapee's "Charmaine." But the real revolution took place the next year when *The Jazz Singer* offered both the sight and the sound of Al Jolson singing and talking. In 1928, Jolson starred in a second popular vehicle, *The Singing Fool*, which found the singer belting out two of his biggest hits, "Sonny Boy" and "I'm Sitting On Top Of The World."

Richard Rodgers and Lorenz Hart

*B*ut the boom years were quickly coming to an end. The so-called "Coolidge prosperity," which continued under President Herbert Hoover, suddenly collapsed on "Black Thursday," October 24, 1929, when the stock market began its five-day plunge that resulted in the loss of over $32 billion worth of equities. By the end of the decade, the horn of plenty was empty as the nation braced itself for the most severe and protracted Depression in its history.

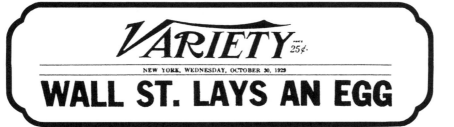

VARIETY PRICE 25¢

NEW YORK, WEDNESDAY, OCTOBER 30, 1929

WALL ST. LAYS AN EGG

The New York Times.

Copyright, 1929, by The New York Times Company.

NEW YORK, TUESDAY, OCTOBER 29, 1929.

STOCK PRICES SLUMP $14,000,000,000 IN NATION-WIDE STAMPEDE TO UNLOAD; BANKERS TO SUPPORT MARKET TODAY

AIN'T MISBEHAVIN'

Words by ANDY RAZAF
Music by THOMAS WALLER and HARRY BROOKS

AMONG MY SOUVENIRS

Words by EDGAR LESLIE
Music by HORATIO NICHOLLS

APRIL SHOWERS

Words by
B.G. DE SYLVA
Music by
LOUIS SILVERS

BABY FACE

Words and Music by BENNY DAVIS
and HARRY AKST

BACK IN YOUR OWN BACK YARD

By AL JOLSON, BILLY ROSE
and DAVE DREYER

THE BEST THINGS IN LIFE ARE FREE

(From "GOOD NEWS")

Music and Lyrics by
B.G. DeSYLVA, LEW BROWN
and RAY HENDERSON

BUTTON UP YOUR OVERCOAT

(From "FOLLOW THRU")

Words and Music by
B.G. DeSYLVA, LEW BROWN
and RAY HENDERSON

CALIFORNIA, HERE I COME

Words and Music by AL JOLSON,
BUD DeSYLVA and JOSEPH MEYER

CHARMAINE

Words and Music by LEW POLLACK
and ERNO RAPEE

COLLEGIATE

By MOE JAFFE
and NAT BONX

Moderately

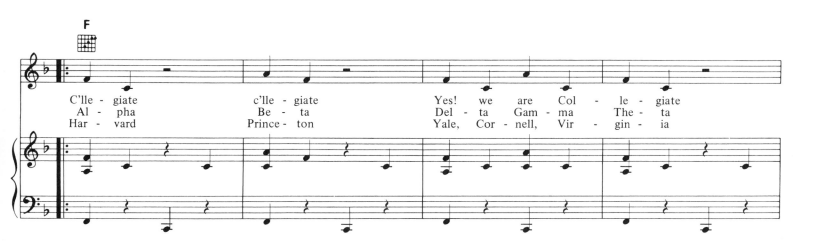

C'lle - giate   c'lle - giate   Yes! we are Col - le - giate
Al - pha   Be - ta   Del - ta Gam - ma The - ta
Har - vard   Prince - ton   Yale, Cor - nell, Vir - gin - ia

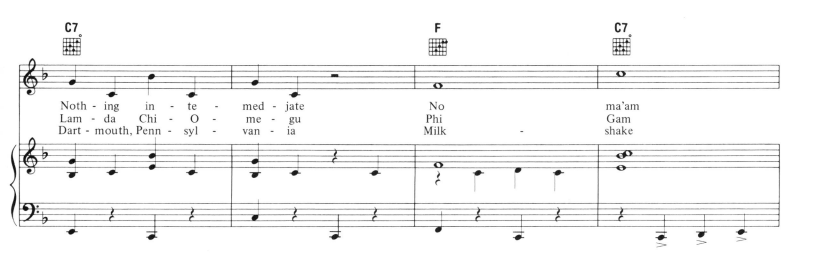

Noth - ing in - te - med - jate   No   ma'am
Lam - da Chi - O - me - gu   Phi   Gam
Dart - mouth, Penn - syl - van - ia   Milk - shake

CRAZY RHYTHM

Words by IRVING CAESAR
Music by JOSEPH MEYER and ROGER WOLFE KAHN

Allegretto moderato

PIANO

I feel like the Em-per-or Ne-ro when Rome was a ve-ry hot
Ev-'ry Greek, each Turk and each La-tin, the Russ-ians and Pruss-ians as

town;
Fath-er Knick-er-bock-er, for-give me, I
well;
When they seek the lure of Man-hat-tan, are

play while your ci-ty burns down;
Through all its night life I
sure to come un-der your spell.
Their na-tive folks songs they

'DEED I DO

Words and Music by
WALTER HIRSCH and FRED ROSE

FIVE FOOT TWO, EYES OF BLUE
(HAS ANYBODY SEEN MY GIRL?)

Words by JOE YOUNG and SAM LEWIS
Music by RAY HENDERSON

EVERYBODY LOVES MY BABY

(But My Baby Don't Love Nobody But Me)

By JACK PALMER & SPENCER WILLIAMS

MCA MUSIC

HALLELUJAH

Words by CLIFFORD GREY and LEO ROBIN
Music by VINCENT YOUMANS

Moderately Bright in 2

mf legato

VERSE

Ebm Ebm7 Fm7-5 Bb7-9 Ebm Fm7-5 Bb7-9

I'm re - call - in' times when I was small in

p

Ebm Abm6 Bb7 Ebm Gb Cb7 Bb7

light and free ju - bi - lee days. _____

Ebm Ebm7 Fm7-5 Bb7-9 Ebm Fm7-5 Bb7-9

Old folks pray - in', ev - 'ry - bod - y sway - in',

HONEYSUCKLE ROSE

Words by ANDY RAZAF
Music by THOMAS ("FATS") WALLER

I CAN'T BELIEVE THAT YOU'RE IN LOVE WITH ME

Words and Music by JIMMY McHUGH
and CLARENCE GASKILL

I CAN'T GIVE YOU ANYTHING BUT LOVE

Words by DOROTHY FIELDS
Music by JIMMY McHUGH

IN A LITTLE SPANISH TOWN
(Twas On A Night Like This)

Words by SAM M. LEWIS and JOE YOUNG
Music by MABEL WAYNE

Chorus, Slowly with much expression

In A Lit - tle Span - ish Town, 'Twas on a night like this,_____

Stars were peek - a - boo - ing down, 'Twas on a night like this,_____

I whis - pered "Be true to me,"_____ And she

sighed: "Si, Si."_____

I CRIED FOR YOU

Words and Music by ARTHUR FREED,
GUS ARNHEIM and ABE LYMAN

I'M SITTING ON TOP OF THE WORLD

Words by SAM M. LEWIS and JOE YOUNG
Music by RAY HENDERSON

IF YOU KNEW SUSIE
(LIKE I KNOW SUSIE)

Words and Music by B.G. DESYLVA
and JOSEPH MEYER

IF YOU WERE
THE ONLY GIRL IN THE WORLD

Words by CLIFFORD GREY
Music by NAT D. AYER

IT ALL DEPENDS ON YOU

Words and Music by
B.G. DeSYLVA, LEW BROWN
and RAY HENDERSON

JEALOUS

Words by TOMMY MALIE and DICK FINCH
Music by JACK LITTLE

LET A SMILE BE YOUR UMBRELLA
(On A Rainy Day)

Words by IRVING KAHAL
and FRANCIS WHEELER
Music by SAMMY FAIN

LOOK FOR THE SILVER LINING

Words by BUD DESYLVA
Music by JEROME KERN

MA
(HE'S MAKING EYES AT ME)

Words by SIDNEY CLARE
Music by CON CONRAD

MAKE BELIEVE
(From "SHOW BOAT")

Words by OSCAR HAMMERSTEIN II
Music by JEROME KERN

MANHATTAN
(From The Broadway Musical "GARRICK GAIETIES")

Words by LORENZ HART
Music by RICHARD RODGERS

Moderately

We'll have Man-hat-tan   The Bronx and Stat-en   Is-land too;_____   It's love-ly
We'll go to Green-wich   Where mod-ern men itch   to be   free;_____   And Bowl-ing
We'll go to Yonk-ers   Where true love con-quers   in the   wilds;_____   And starve to-
We'll have Man-hat-tan   The Bronx and Stat-en   Is-land too;_____   We'll try to

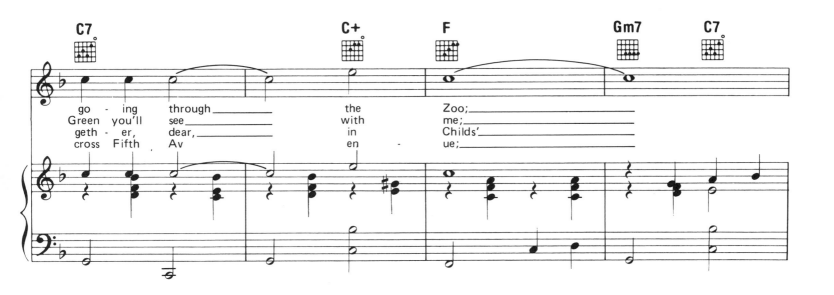

go-ing   through_____   the   Zoo;_____
Green you'll see_____   with   me;_____
geth-er, dear,_____   in   Childs'_____
cross Fifth   Av   en-   ue;_____

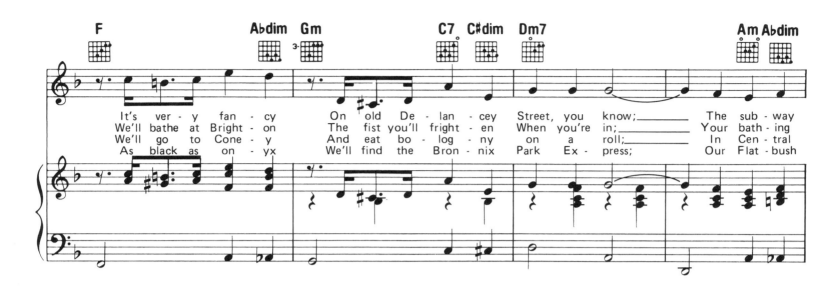

It's ver - y fan - cy | On old De - lan - cey | Street, you know;_____ The sub - way
We'll bathe at Bright - on | The fist you'll fright - en | When you're in;_____ Your bath - ing
We'll go to Cone - y | And eat bo - log - ny | on a roll;_____ In Cen - tral
As black as on - yx | We'll find the Bron - nix | Park Ex - press;_____ Our Flat - bush

charms us so,_____ When balm - y | breez - es blow | to and fro; | And tell me what street
suit so thin_____ Will make the | shell - fish grin | Fin to fin; | I'd like to take a
Park, we'll stroll_____ Where our first | kiss we stole, | Soul to soul; | And for some high fare
flat, I guess_____ Will be a | great suc - cess. | More or less; | A short va - ca - tion

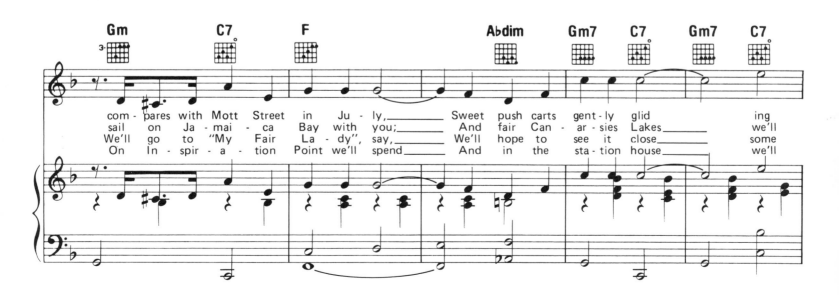

com - pares with Mott | Street in Ju - ly,_____ Sweet push carts gent - ly glid - | ing
sail on Ja - mai - ca | Bay with you;_____ And fair Can - ar - sies Lakes_____ we'll
On In - spir - a - tion | Point we'll spend_____ And in the sta - tion house_____ we'll

ME AND MY SHADOW

Words by BILLY ROSE
Music by AL JOLSON and DAVE DREYER

MEAN TO ME

Words and Music by FRED E. AHLERT
and ROY TURK

101

MISS YOU

Words by CHARLES TOBIAS
and HARRY TOBIAS
Music by HENRY H. TOBIAS

MISSISSIPPI MUD

By JAMES CAVANAUGH and HARRY BARRIS

PADDLIN' MADELIN' HOME

Words and Music by
HARRY WOODS

MOONLIGHT AND ROSES
(Bring Mem'ries Of You)

Words and Music by BEN BLACK,
EDWIN H. LEMARE and NEIL MORET

MORE THAN YOU KNOW

Slowly, With Expression

Words by WILLIAM ROSE and EDWARD ELISCU
Music by VINCENT YOUMANS

MY MAMMY

Words by SAM M. LEWIS
and JOE YOUNG
Music by WALTER DONALDSON

OL' MAN RIVER

(From "SHOW BOAT")

Words by OSCAR HAMMERSTEIN II
Music by JEROME KERN

SECOND HAND ROSE

Words by GRANT CLARKE
Music by JAMES F. HANLEY

SENTIMENTAL ME

Words by JIMMY CASSIN
Music by JIM MOREHEAD

THE SHEIK OF ARABY

Words by HARRY B. SMITH
and FRANCIS WHEELER
Music by TED SNYDER

SIDE BY SIDE

Words and Music by
HARRY WOODS

SONNY BOY

Words and Music by AL JOLSON,
B.G. DeSYLVA, LEW BROWN
and RAY HENDERSON

1. Climb up-on my knee, Son-ny boy; You are on-ly three, Son-ny boy.
2. You're my dear-est prize, Son-ny boy; Sent from out the skies, Son-ny boy.

You've no way of know-ing there's no way of show-ing
Let me hold you near-er One thing makes you dear-er:

What you mean to me, Son-ny boy.
You've your moth-ers eyes, Son-ny boy.

STAR DUST

Words by MITCHELL PARISH
Music by HOAGY CARMICHAEL

SUGAR BLUES

Words by LUCY FLETCHER
Music by CLARENCE WILLIAMS

THERE'LL BE SOME CHANGES MADE

Words by BILLY HIGGINS
Music by W. BENTON OVERSTREET

D7
G7
chang - ing jokes, I must make some chang - es from old to the new
C9
C7
F7
G7
I must do things just the same as oth - ers do, I'm goin' to change my long, tall 'Mam - ma / Dad - dy for a
C9
lit - tle short Fat, Goin' to change the num - ber where I live at. I
D7
G7
C9
F7
must have some lov - in' or I'll fade a - way, There'll be some chang - es
B♭
A♭7
G7
C9
F7
B♭
made to - day There'll Be Some Chang - es Made.

TOGETHER

Words and Music by B.G. DeSYLVA,
RAY HENDERSON and LEW BROWN

Moderately Slow

THE VARSITY DRAG

(From "GOOD NEWS")

Words and Music by B. G. DeSYLVA,
LEW BROWN and RAY HENDERSON

THE WANG WANG BLUES

Words and Music by LEO WOOD, GUS MUELLER,
BUSTER JOHNSON and HENRY BUSSE

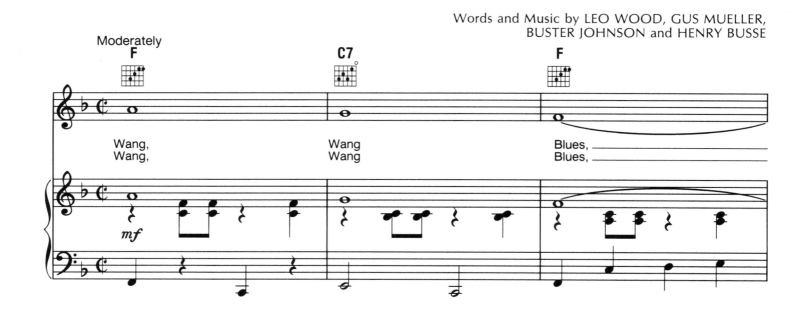

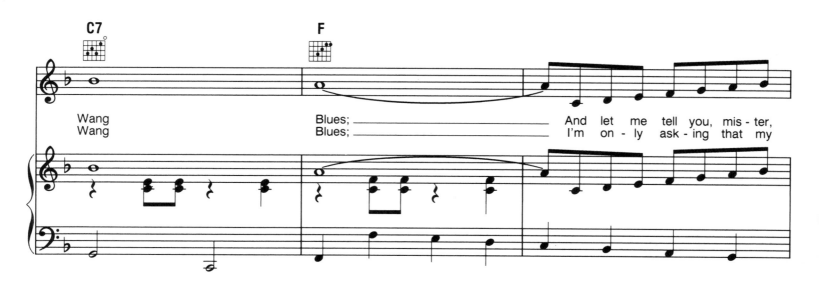

'WAY DOWN YONDER IN NEW ORLEANS

By HENRY CREAMER and J. TURNER LAYTON

Way Down Yon - der In New Or - leans___ In the land___ of dream-y scenes___

There's a gar - den of E - den That's what I mean,___ Cre - ole ba - bies with

flash - ing eyes___ Soft - ly whis - per with ten - der sighs___ "Stop! Oh! won't you

WEDDING BELLS
(Are Breaking Up That Old Gang Of Mine)

Words by IRVING KAHAL
and WILLI RASKIN
Music by SAMMY FAIN

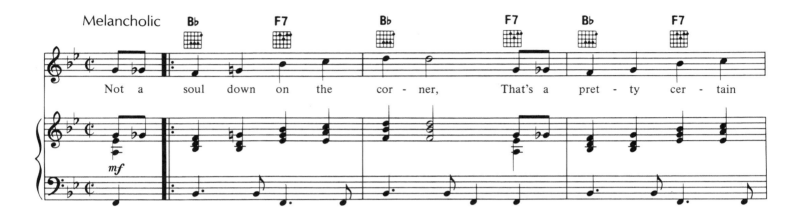

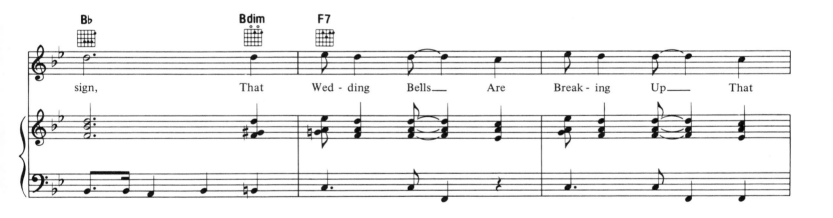

WHEN MY SUGAR WALKS DOWN THE STREET
(All The Little Birdies Go Tweet-Tweet-Tweet)

Words and Music by GENE AUSTIN,
JIMMIE McHUGH AND IRVING MILLS

With a beat

WHEN THE RED, RED ROBIN COMES BOB, BOB BOBBIN' ALONG

By HARRY WOODS

WHEN YOU'RE SMILING
(THE WHOLE WORLD SMILES WITH YOU)

By MARK FISHER, JOE GOODWIN
& LARRY SHAY

Moderately

When you're smil - ing, _____ when you're smil - ing, _____ the

whole world smiles with you, _____ when you're laugh - ing, _____

_____ When you're laugh - ing _____ The sun comes shin - ing

YEARNING

Words and Music by BENNY DAVIS
and JOE BURKE

YES! WE HAVE NO BANANAS

By FRANK SILVER and IRVING COHN

You're The Cream In My Coffee

(From "HOLD EVERYTHING")

Words & Music by B.G. DeSYLVA,
LEW BROWN & RAY HENDERSON

WHO'S SORRY NOW

Words by BERT KALMAR & HARRY RUBY
Music by TED SNYDER